GALAXY S25 ULTRA SIMPLIFIED

A Complete User's Handbook to Navigate Features, Settings, and Troubleshooting Like a Pro. From Setup to Advanced Tips

Avery Tech

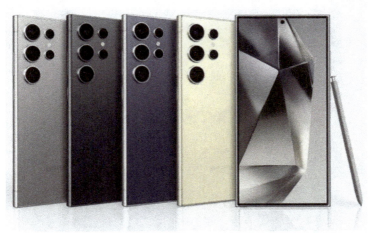

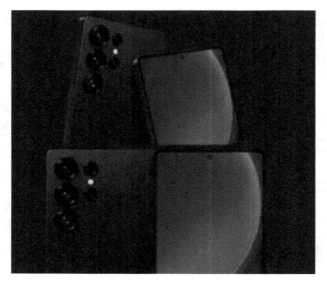

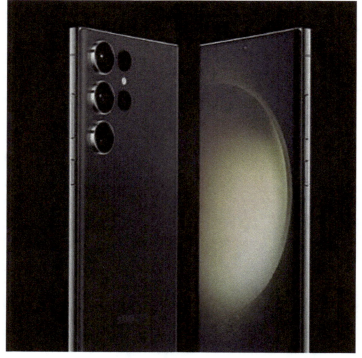

SAMSUNG GALAXY S24 ULTRA TECH SPECS SUMMARY

The Samsung Galaxy S24 Ultra is a flagship smartphone that combines cutting-edge technology with elegant design, offering users a premium mobile experience. Here's a concise overview of its key technical specifications:

Display:

- 6.8-inch Dynamic LTPO AMOLED 2X
- 1440 x 3120 resolution (505 ppi)
- 120Hz refresh rate
- HDR10+ support
- Peak brightness up to 2600 nits

Processor:

- Qualcomm Snapdragon 8 Gen 3 (4 nm)
- Octa-core CPU configuration
- Adreno 750 GPU

Memory and Storage Options:

- 12GB RAM
- Storage variants: 256GB, 512GB, 1TB

- No microSD card slot for expandable storage

Camera System:

- *Rear Cameras:*
    - 200 MP main sensor (f/1.7, 24mm, OIS)
    - 10 MP telephoto lens (f/2.4, 3x optical zoom, OIS)
    - 50 MP periscope telephoto lens (f/3.4, 5x optical zoom, OIS)
    - 12 MP ultra-wide lens (f/2.2, 120° field of view)
- *Front Camera:*
    - 12 MP sensor (f/2.2, 26mm)

Battery and Charging:

- 5000mAh non-removable battery
- 45W wired charging (PD3.0)
- 15W wireless charging (Qi/PMA)
- 4.5W reverse wireless charging

Build and Design:

- Dimensions: 162.3 x 79 x 8.6 mm
- Weight: Approximately 232g
- Materials: Gorilla Glass front and back, titanium frame

- IP68 dust and water resistance
- Integrated S Pen with Bluetooth support

Operating System:

- Android 14
- Samsung's One UI 6.1.1

Connectivity:

- 5G support
- Wi-Fi 802.11 a/b/g/n/ac/6e/7
- Bluetooth 5.3
- NFC
- USB Type-C 3.2
- Ultra Wideband (UWB) support

Additional Features:

- Under-display ultrasonic fingerprint sensor
- Stereo speakers tuned by AKG
- No 3.5mm headphone jack
- Available in multiple color options, including Titanium Black, Gray, Violet, Yellow, Blue, Green, and Orange

The Galaxy S24 Ultra stands out with its advanced camera capabilities, robust performance, and a vibrant display, making it a top choice for users seeking a high-end smartphone experience.

INTRODUCTION

Welcome to your journey with the Galaxy S25 Ultra—a smartphone that not only pushes the boundaries of technology but also redefines how we connect, create, and explore every day. Whether you're a seasoned tech enthusiast or new to the world of premium smartphones, this guide is designed to be your trusted companion every step of the way.

Who This Guide Is For

This handbook is for anyone eager to unlock the full potential of the Galaxy S25 Ultra. If you're just unboxing your device for the first time, or if you're looking to dive deep into its advanced features, this book has something for you. We've tailored it for everyday users who appreciate clear instructions and practical advice, as well as for tech-savvy professionals seeking advanced tips and troubleshooting strategies.

What's New in the Galaxy S25 Ultra

The Galaxy S25 Ultra isn't just another upgrade—it's a revolution in design and performance. With groundbreaking innovations such as an ultra-high resolution camera, enhanced battery management, a more intuitive user interface, and powerful connectivity features, this device sets a new standard for what a smartphone can do. Expect improvements that make everyday tasks simpler and creative endeavors more exciting, all while delivering a smooth, user-friendly experience.

How to Use This Handbook

This guide is structured to help you progress naturally from the basics to the more advanced aspects of your new device. We start with everything you need for that first unboxing and setup, and gradually move on to exploring the sophisticated features like the S Pen, camera settings, and personalized customization options. Each chapter is packed with step-by-step instructions, tips, and troubleshooting advice, ensuring that you can easily reference a topic whenever you need help or inspiration. Think of it as a roadmap to mastering your Galaxy S25 Ultra— designed to make your experience as seamless and enjoyable as possible.

Dive in, explore, and most importantly, enjoy every moment with your Galaxy S25 Ultra!

CHAPTER ONE

Unboxing and First-Time Setup

Welcome to the exciting start of your journey with the Galaxy S25 Ultra! In this chapter, we'll walk through every step of your first encounter with this innovative device—from the moment you open the box to transferring your precious memories from your old phone. Let's dive in and make your setup experience as smooth and enjoyable as possible.

What's Inside the Box

When you open the Galaxy S25 Ultra package, you're greeted with a sleek design and thoughtful organization. Inside, you'll typically find:

- **Your Galaxy S25 Ultra:** Nestled securely in a custom-molded slot that protects it during transit.

- **Charging Accessories:** A fast charger and a USB-C cable to get you powered up quickly.

- **Documentation:** Quick start guides, warranty information, and safety instructions to help you get acquainted with your new device.

- **Additional Accessories:** Depending on your region and package, you might also discover extra items like earbuds or a SIM card ejector tool.

Take a moment to admire the care and attention to detail. This unboxing experience isn't just about revealing a new gadget—it's the first step into a world of cutting-edge technology that's designed to simplify and enrich your everyday life.

Charging and Powering On

Before you can explore the fantastic features of the Galaxy S25 Ultra, you need to give it some life. Here's how to get started:

1. **Charge Your Device:**

   o **Why It's Important:** A fully charged device ensures that you have enough power for the initial setup and all the exciting features ahead.

   o **How to Do It:** Plug the provided USB-C cable into the charger and connect it to your phone. A battery icon or a welcome screen should appear, confirming that your device is charging.

2. **Powering On:**

   o Once you're confident that your phone has enough juice, press and hold the power button until you see the Samsung logo. This marks the beginning of your journey with the Galaxy S25 Ultra.

This simple process not only prepares your device for use but also gives you a chance to feel the quality and responsiveness of your new smartphone.

Initial Setup: Language, Wi-Fi, and Accounts

After powering on, you'll be guided through the initial setup process. This step is crucial for personalizing your device and connecting it to the digital world. Here's what to expect:

1. **Language Selection:**

   o Choose your preferred language from the list provided. This setting will be the foundation of your interaction with the device, so take a moment to pick the one you're most comfortable with.

2. **Connecting to Wi-Fi:**

o **Why It Matters:** A stable internet connection is essential for downloading updates, syncing your data, and accessing online services.

o **How to Connect:** Select your Wi-Fi network from the available list, enter the password, and confirm the connection. The setup assistant will test the connection to ensure everything is working smoothly.

3. **Signing In to Your Accounts:**

o **Google and Samsung Accounts:** To fully enjoy the benefits of the Galaxy S25 Ultra, you'll need to sign in to your Google and Samsung accounts. This step allows you to access the Google Play Store, Samsung's ecosystem of apps, cloud backups, and more.

o **Customization and Security:** As you sign in, you may also be prompted to set up security features like fingerprint recognition or facial recognition. These features are designed to keep your data safe and ensure that only you have access to your device.

Following these steps ensures that your Galaxy S25 Ultra is personalized and ready for your daily tasks. The process is designed to be intuitive and user-friendly, so you can focus on exploring the device rather than getting bogged down in technical details.

Transferring Data from an Old Device

One of the most exciting parts of getting a new phone is bringing your favorite apps, photos, contacts, and settings along for the ride. The Galaxy S25 Ultra offers several methods for a seamless data transfer:

1. **Smart Switch:**

    o **What It Does:** Samsung's Smart Switch is a powerful tool that allows you to transfer data from your old phone to your new Galaxy S25 Ultra effortlessly.

    o **How to Use It:** Install the Smart Switch app on both your old device and your new phone. Follow the on-screen instructions to connect the devices—either wirelessly or using a cable—and choose the data you wish to transfer. The app will guide you through every step, ensuring that your contacts, photos, apps, and more find their new home on your Galaxy S25 Ultra.

2. **Cloud Backups:**

   o If you have previously backed up your data to a cloud service (like Google Drive or Samsung Cloud), you can restore these backups during the initial setup. This method ensures that even if you switch devices frequently, your data stays with you.

3. **Manual Transfer:**

   o For those who prefer a hands-on approach, you can also manually move files using a computer or external storage. While this method may take a bit longer, it gives you complete control over what data is transferred.

By transferring your data, you're not just setting up a new device—you're carrying forward your digital life. This step ensures that your new Galaxy S25 Ultra feels familiar right from the start, with all your important information readily available.

Taking the time to unbox and set up your Galaxy S25 Ultra properly is an investment in your future experience with the device. This chapter has provided a comprehensive, step-by-step guide to ensure that your first interactions are smooth and stress-free. As you move forward, remember that every feature and setting is designed to make your life easier, more connected, and a lot more fun.

Now that your Galaxy S25 Ultra is up and running, get ready to explore the rich user interface and innovative features in the upcoming chapters. Welcome to the future of smart technology—welcome to your new digital companion!

CHAPTER TWO

Understanding the User Interface

Welcome to Chapter 2! Now that your Galaxy S25 Ultra is set up and ready, it's time to get acquainted with its heart and soul— the user interface. In this chapter, we'll take a closer look at Samsung's latest version of One UI and explore the different navigation options available, so you can find the method that fits you best.

Exploring One UI (Samsung's Latest Version)

One UI is much more than just an attractive design; it's a thoughtfully crafted experience that prioritizes ease of use and personalization. Samsung has designed One UI to simplify your interactions and make every task feel natural. Here are some highlights:

- **Intuitive Layout:** One UI features a clean, organized layout with larger icons and ample spacing. This means you can easily locate your favorite apps and settings without feeling overwhelmed.

- **Personalized Experience:** Whether you're a fan of dark mode, enjoy dynamic themes, or like arranging widgets exactly how you want them, One UI adapts to your preferences and lifestyle.

- **Enhanced Accessibility:** The design is user-friendly for everyone. With features like high contrast mode and adjustable font sizes, One UI ensures that all users have a comfortable experience.

- **Seamless Integration:** One UI works harmoniously with Samsung's ecosystem, meaning your device easily connects with other Samsung services and products, providing a smooth, integrated experience.

Samsung's continuous refinements to One UI mean that your Galaxy S25 Ultra not only looks modern and elegant but also works intuitively, making everyday tasks easier and more enjoyable.

Navigation Gestures vs. Button Navigation

Samsung understands that every user is unique. That's why your Galaxy S25 Ultra offers two primary navigation methods: sleek navigation gestures and traditional button navigation. Each has its own advantages, so you can choose the one that suits your style best.

Navigation Gestures

- **Modern and Immersive:** Gestures let you enjoy a full-screen experience without the distraction of visible buttons. This design maximizes your display, giving you more space for your apps and content.

- **Fluid and Natural:** Swiping and tapping feel intuitive, making transitions between apps and menus seamless. Once you get the hang of it, navigating via gestures can be both fast and enjoyable.

- **Customizable Actions:** You can tailor many gestures to your liking. Whether it's swiping up to view all your apps or using specific motions for multitasking, gestures provide a flexible way to interact with your device.

- **A Short Learning Curve:** While it might take a little time to master these gestures, most users quickly find that they enhance their overall experience by providing a more dynamic way to control their phone.

Button Navigation

- **Familiar and Reliable:** For many, the traditional layout of fixed on-screen buttons—home, back, and recent apps—offers a sense of comfort and familiarity. It's a tried-and-true method that feels straightforward.

- **Consistent Access:** With button navigation, you always have visible, dedicated controls. This can be especially handy in situations where you need a quick, unmistakable way to return to your home screen.

- **Ideal for Accessibility:** Some users prefer the tactile reassurance of buttons, particularly if gestures feel less intuitive or if accessibility needs call for a more static setup.

Choosing Your Navigation Style

The best part is that switching between these two navigation styles is simple, allowing you to experiment and settle on the method that feels most natural to you. Whether you choose the modern fluidity of gestures or the steady dependability of buttons, your Galaxy S25 Ultra is designed to offer a user-friendly experience tailored to your personal habits.

Home Screen Customization

Your home screen is your personal launchpad—a space that's entirely yours. With the Galaxy S25 Ultra, you have the freedom to design it just the way you like it. Here's how to make it uniquely yours:

- **Personal Touch with Wallpapers and Themes:** Start by setting a wallpaper that speaks to you. Whether it's a stunning landscape, abstract art, or a snapshot of a cherished memory, your background sets the tone. You can also explore themes that change icons, colors, and even the overall mood of your device.

- **Widgets: Your Mini-Apps on Display:** Widgets bring your favorite information to your fingertips. From weather updates and calendar events to quick access to your music player, widgets are designed to keep you informed without the need to open an app. Arrange them on your home screen so that your most-used information is always within view.

- **Organize with Folders:** Don't let a cluttered screen slow you down. Group similar apps into folders to keep everything organized. For instance, you might create a folder for social media apps, another for productivity tools, and yet another for entertainment. This not only declutters your view but also speeds up your navigation.

- **Customize the Layout:** Samsung's One UI offers flexible grid sizes, allowing you to adjust the number of app icons and widgets on your screen. Play around with the layout until it feels just right—whether you prefer a minimalist look or a dynamic, information-rich display.

- **Experiment and Evolve:** Your home screen isn't set in stone. As your habits and needs change, feel free to experiment with new arrangements, remove what no longer works, and add fresh elements that enhance your experience. The Galaxy S25 Ultra is designed to adapt as you do.

By tailoring your home screen, you're not only making your device look great, but you're also creating a workflow that's as efficient as it is personal. It's about crafting an environment that feels intuitive and truly yours.

Quick Settings and Notifications

In today's fast-paced world, quick access to essential settings and timely notifications is key to staying connected and productive. Let's look at how the Galaxy S25 Ultra's Quick Settings and Notifications panels work to keep you in control:

- **Accessing Quick Settings:** With a simple swipe from the top of your screen, you open the Quick Settings panel—a customizable menu that puts vital toggles at your fingertips. Here, you can turn on Wi-Fi, adjust screen brightness, activate battery saver mode, and much more. It's all about reducing the number of steps needed to get things done.

- **Customizing Quick Settings:** Not all settings are created equal for every user. The Galaxy S25 Ultra lets you rearrange and personalize these shortcuts. Tap the edit icon (usually a pencil or similar symbol), and drag your most-used settings to the top. Remove those that you rarely need, and add any extra shortcuts that would enhance your daily routine.

- **Notifications: Your Personalized Alerts:** Notifications keep you informed without demanding constant attention. Whether it's an important email, a calendar reminder, or a social media update, notifications appear in a dedicated panel when you swipe down from the top of your screen. They're designed to be concise, providing just enough information for you to decide whether to act immediately or deal with it later.

- **Managing Your Notifications:** Too many notifications can be overwhelming. Fortunately, the Galaxy S25 Ultra gives you tools to manage them. You can set priorities for different apps, group similar notifications, and even choose to snooze non-urgent alerts. This way, your device stays informative without becoming a distraction.

- **Interactive and Contextual Controls:** Some notifications come with interactive options. For example, you might respond directly to a message or control media playback right from the notification shade. These features ensure that you can act quickly and efficiently, without needing to open the full app.

By mastering Quick Settings and Notifications, you'll find that everyday tasks become smoother and more intuitive. Whether you're quickly switching to airplane mode before boarding a flight or catching up on your schedule with a glance, these tools are all about enhancing your control and efficiency.

Understanding and personalizing your Galaxy S25 Ultra's user interface is more than just a technical exercise—it's about crafting a digital space that works for you. From the moment you arrange your home screen to the way you manage your quick settings and notifications, every choice you make enhances your overall experience. Embrace the flexibility, explore the customization options, and soon your device will feel not only high-tech but also truly personal.

Now that you're familiar with these essential elements, you're one step closer to mastering the full potential of your Galaxy S25 Ultra. Enjoy the journey of making this powerful tool uniquely yours!

CHAPTER THREE

Mastering Calls, Messages, and Contacts

Effective communication is at the heart of your daily interactions, and with the Galaxy S25 Ultra, staying connected has never been easier or more efficient. In this chapter, we'll explore how to make and receive calls, manage your contacts effortlessly, and take advantage of advanced messaging features. Whether you're making a quick call or engaging in a rich, multimedia conversation, these tools are designed to keep you connected with ease and style.

Making and Receiving Calls

Your Galaxy S25 Ultra is equipped with a robust calling system that transforms every call into a seamless experience. Here's how to make the most out of its calling features:

- **Placing Calls with Ease:**

  - **Dialing Made Simple:** Open the Phone app to access the dial pad. Simply tap the numbers or select a contact from your list, and you're just a tap away from a conversation.

o **Voice Command Integration:** For hands-free convenience, use voice commands by activating Bixby or your preferred voice assistant. Just say, "Call [Contact Name]," and the device will handle the rest.

- **Receiving Calls Smoothly:**

  o **Clear Caller Information:** When a call comes in, you'll see the caller's name, photo, or even their location if you've set it up. This helps you decide whether to answer or let the call go to voicemail.

  o **Managing In-Call Options:** Once connected, you have a suite of in-call features at your fingertips—mute, speakerphone, hold, and even call recording (where supported and permitted). These options ensure that your calls are not only clear but also tailored to your specific needs.

- **Staying in Control:**

  o **Call History and Voicemail:** Easily access your call history to redial missed numbers or review recent calls. Integrated voicemail services ensure you never miss important messages.

By streamlining the process of making and receiving calls, the Galaxy S25 Ultra ensures that every conversation is smooth, whether you're catching up with friends or handling important business matters.

Managing Contacts Efficiently

A well-organized contacts list is essential for efficient communication. Your Galaxy S25 Ultra provides a host of features to help you keep your contacts neat and accessible:

- **Adding and Editing Contacts:**

    - **Quick Entry:** Easily add new contacts directly from a call, message, or via the dedicated Contacts app. Update details like phone numbers, email addresses, and even photos to give each contact a personal touch.

    - **Smart Integration:** The device seamlessly syncs with your Google or Samsung account, ensuring your contacts are always backed up and available across all your devices.

- **Organizing Contacts:**

    - **Groups and Favorites:** Create groups (like family, friends, or work) for faster access during calls and messaging. Mark frequently contacted individuals as favorites for instant dialing.

- ○ **Merging Duplicates:** Over time, duplicate entries might accumulate. The Galaxy S25 Ultra can automatically detect and merge duplicate contacts, keeping your list clutter-free.

- **Advanced Management Tools:**

  - ○ **Search and Filter:** Quickly locate a contact with a built-in search function. Filter your list by groups or labels to find exactly what you need in seconds.

  - ○ **Secure Sharing:** Easily share contact information via NFC, email, or messaging apps without compromising security.

By keeping your contacts well-organized, you create a more efficient and stress-free communication environment, making it simpler to reach the people who matter most.

Advanced Messaging Features

Messaging on the Galaxy S25 Ultra goes beyond basic text—it's about rich, interactive, and smart communication that adapts to your lifestyle:

- **Enhanced Messaging Experience:**

  o **Rich Communication Services (RCS):** Enjoy a messaging experience that supports high-resolution photos, videos, and even group chats with live location sharing. RCS brings your texts to life, allowing for more engaging conversations.

  o **Smart Replies:** Benefit from context-aware suggestions that let you reply quickly without typing lengthy responses. This feature uses AI to offer tailored reply options based on the conversation.

- **Interactive and Multimedia Messaging:**

  o **Voice and Video Messaging:** Sometimes words aren't enough. Record and send voice messages or start a quick video call directly from the messaging interface.

  o **Multimedia Integration:** Share documents, images, and even your favorite GIFs with ease. The interface makes it simple to switch between text, voice, and multimedia messages without missing a beat.

- **Customization and Privacy:**

    o **Message Organization:** Archive, pin, or mute conversations to prioritize what matters most. This keeps your messaging app uncluttered and focused on your current needs.

    o **Security and Encryption:** Advanced security features ensure that your messages remain private and protected, giving you peace of mind with every conversation.

With these advanced messaging features, your Galaxy S25 Ultra transforms the way you communicate, making every message more engaging, efficient, and secure.

Mastering calls, messages, and contacts on your Galaxy S25 Ultra is about more than just functionality—it's about creating a seamless communication experience tailored to your lifestyle. By making and receiving calls effortlessly, managing your contacts with precision, and leveraging advanced messaging features, you're well-equipped to stay connected in a way that's both smart and personal.

Embrace these tools, experiment with the features, and soon you'll find that your Galaxy S25 Ultra isn't just a phone—it's an essential partner in your daily communication. Happy connecting!

CHAPTER FOUR

Internet, Connectivity, and Smart Features

In our fast-paced digital world, staying connected is more than a convenience—it's essential. Your Galaxy S25 Ultra is engineered to keep you online, link you seamlessly with other devices, and even transform your phone into a desktop-like experience. In this chapter, we'll explore how to set up mobile data and Wi-Fi, harness the power of Bluetooth and NFC for effortless sharing, and dive into the smart world of Samsung DeX and wireless connectivity. Let's get connected and explore the possibilities!

Setting Up Mobile Data and Wi-Fi

Staying online wherever you are starts with a solid internet connection. Whether you're commuting, at home, or on the go, your Galaxy S25 Ultra ensures you're always connected.

- **Mobile Data – Freedom on the Go:**

  - **Activation Made Easy:** Begin by accessing your settings and navigating to the "Connections" section. Here, you can toggle mobile data on or off with a single tap. If you're new to the device, you might need to select your preferred network mode (like 5G or LTE) based on your carrier's support.

- o **Managing Data Usage:** It's not just about being online; it's about using your data wisely. Set data limits and alerts to help you monitor usage, ensuring you never exceed your plan. This is especially useful for those who work remotely or travel frequently.

- **Wi-Fi – Your Home and Office Hub:**

  - o **Simple Connection Process:** To connect to Wi-Fi, swipe down from the top of your screen to access the Quick Settings panel, then tap the Wi-Fi icon. Choose your network from the list, enter the password if prompted, and you're set.

  - o **Staying Secure:** Always opt for secure, password-protected networks. Your device will also notify you if it detects an unsecured network, helping you keep your data safe.

  - o **Smart Connectivity:** With advanced features, the Galaxy S25 Ultra can automatically switch between Wi-Fi and mobile data to maintain the best possible connection. This means you can enjoy uninterrupted streaming, browsing, or work, without manual intervention.

By setting up your mobile data and Wi-Fi correctly, you create a solid foundation for all other smart features, ensuring that you're always connected no matter where life takes you.

Using Bluetooth and NFC

Once you're online, connecting with nearby devices and sharing content becomes the next exciting step. The Galaxy S25 Ultra offers versatile options like Bluetooth and NFC, each with its unique benefits.

- **Bluetooth – Wireless Connection Redefined:**

  o **Pairing with Ease:** Bluetooth is perfect for connecting your wireless headphones, speakers, car systems, or even other smart devices. Simply go to your Bluetooth settings, toggle it on, and let your phone search for nearby devices. Once your device appears in the list, tap to pair—it's that simple.

  o **Versatile Sharing:** Beyond audio, Bluetooth can be used for sharing files, photos, or even apps between devices. This seamless connectivity allows you to quickly transfer information without the need for cables.

o **Energy Efficiency:** Modern Bluetooth technology is designed to use less power, so you can enjoy extended battery life while staying connected with your favorite peripherals.

- **NFC (Near Field Communication) – Tap and Connect:**

  o **Instant Interactions:** NFC takes connectivity to another level by allowing your phone to communicate with other NFC-enabled devices or payment terminals with just a tap. Whether you're sharing a contact, paying for groceries, or connecting to a compatible speaker, NFC makes these transactions quick and secure.

  o **Simplified Setup:** Activating NFC is as easy as a swipe through your settings. Once enabled, you'll find that transferring information or making payments is practically instantaneous, removing the friction from everyday transactions.

  o **Secure by Design:** NFC transactions are highly secure, making them ideal for sensitive actions like mobile payments or accessing secure areas with digital keys.

Using Bluetooth and NFC ensures that your Galaxy S25 Ultra doesn't exist in isolation—it becomes a central hub in a network of devices, each interaction enhancing your digital experience.

Samsung DeX and Wireless Connectivity

Imagine transforming your smartphone into a desktop computer without the hassle of wires. With Samsung DeX and wireless connectivity features, your Galaxy S25 Ultra opens up a world of productivity and flexibility.

- **Samsung DeX – Desktop Experience on the Go:**

  - **What Is DeX?** Samsung DeX is a powerful tool that lets you connect your phone to a larger display—be it a monitor, TV, or even a compatible laptop—turning your mobile device into a fully functional desktop workstation.

  - **Getting Started:** Setting up DeX is intuitive. You can connect via a cable, or even opt for wireless DeX, which lets you mirror your phone's screen on your TV or monitor without a single wire. Once connected, you'll see a familiar desktop interface with resizable windows, a taskbar, and keyboard support.

o **Boosting Productivity:** DeX enables you to run multiple apps side-by-side, manage files with ease, and even edit documents with a full keyboard and mouse. Whether you're preparing a presentation, multitasking on several projects, or just browsing, DeX transforms your workflow into a more expansive and efficient experience.

- **Wireless Connectivity – Freedom from Cables:**

o **Screen Mirroring and Casting:** With wireless connectivity, you can effortlessly share your phone's screen with compatible smart TVs and displays. This is perfect for streaming movies, presenting slides, or even gaming on a bigger screen.

o **Seamless Integration:** The Galaxy S25 Ultra's wireless features are designed for minimal setup and maximum flexibility. Whether you're using Miracast, Wi-Fi Direct, or other wireless protocols, connecting to external devices is smooth and fast.

o **Enhanced Mobility:** Gone are the days of being tethered to a cable. With wireless connectivity, you have the freedom to work, play, and share content from anywhere in your home or office without sacrificing performance.

Samsung DeX and wireless connectivity not only extend the capabilities of your Galaxy S25 Ultra but also empower you to transform your smartphone into a versatile tool—be it for work, entertainment, or creative projects.

Connecting to the digital world has never been easier, thanks to the Galaxy S25 Ultra's robust connectivity and smart features. From setting up your mobile data and Wi-Fi for a reliable internet connection, to using Bluetooth and NFC for effortless sharing, and finally, to leveraging Samsung DeX and wireless connectivity for a desktop-like experience—the possibilities are endless.

As you experiment with these features, you'll find that your device adapts perfectly to your lifestyle, keeping you connected in every sense of the word. Enjoy the journey, explore these capabilities, and let your Galaxy S25 Ultra enhance every aspect of your digital experience!

CHAPTER FIVE

Mastering the S Pen

The S Pen is more than just a stylus—it's your creative partner, your quick-access remote, and a tool that makes your Galaxy S25 Ultra truly versatile. In this chapter, we'll explore the many features of the S Pen, show you how to customize it to suit your unique style, and reveal the magic behind converting your handwriting into text. Whether you're jotting down ideas, editing photos, or navigating your device, the S Pen is here to enhance every experience.

S Pen Features and Customization

The S Pen offers a world of possibilities right at your fingertips. Here's how to make the most of its features and tailor it to your needs:

- **Intuitive Air Actions:** Experience the freedom of controlling your device from a distance. With air actions, you can swipe through photos, scroll documents, or even launch apps with simple gestures. This hands-free functionality is perfect for busy moments or when you're on the go.

- **Screen Off Memo:** Capture ideas as soon as they strike—even when your screen is off. Just pull out the S Pen and start writing a quick note. It's like having a digital notepad that's always ready for inspiration.

- **Customizable Shortcuts:** Personalize your S Pen's buttons to perform actions you use most. Whether you want to open your camera app, take a screenshot, or launch a specific note-taking app, you can assign shortcuts that make your workflow smoother and more efficient.

- **Pressure Sensitivity and Precision:** With enhanced pressure sensitivity, the S Pen responds to the lightest touch and provides a natural writing experience. Perfect for drawing, editing photos, or marking up documents, it adapts to your every move, ensuring accuracy whether you're doodling or annotating a report.

- **S Pen Settings:** Dive into the settings menu to adjust the sensitivity, customize gestures, and explore additional features. Samsung's One UI makes it easy to experiment and find the perfect configuration that matches your style. With a few taps, you can switch between modes and features, ensuring the S Pen works exactly how you want it to.

By exploring these features and taking the time to customize the S Pen, you transform it from a simple accessory into a powerful extension of your creativity and productivity.

Detail antenna description

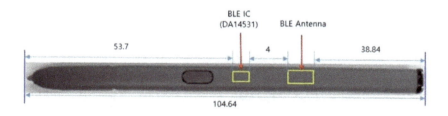

Handwriting to Text

Imagine the convenience of writing down your thoughts by hand and having them magically transformed into digital text. The Galaxy S25 Ultra makes this a reality with its seamless handwriting-to-text conversion. Here's how you can take advantage of this feature:

- **Writing Naturally:** Start by opening an app that supports handwriting input, like Samsung Notes. With the S Pen in hand, write as you normally would. The device's advanced recognition technology captures every stroke, whether it's a quick note or a detailed paragraph.

- **Converting Handwritten Notes:** Once you've finished writing, simply select the option to convert your handwriting into text. The conversion is designed to be intuitive and accurate, preserving your natural writing style while transforming it into editable text. This feature is perfect for creating quick drafts, composing emails, or even jotting down to-do lists without having to type them out manually.

- **Editing and Sharing:** After conversion, you can easily edit the text to ensure it's perfect. Once you're happy with it, share your note via email, messaging apps, or save it for later reference. This seamless transition from handwritten to digital means you can focus on your ideas rather than getting bogged down by typing.

- **Practical Uses:** Whether you're in a meeting, class, or brainstorming session, converting handwriting to text can speed up your workflow. It's an invaluable tool for anyone who loves the organic feel of handwriting but needs the convenience and efficiency of digital text.

Mastering the S Pen unlocks a new level of creativity and efficiency on your Galaxy S25 Ultra. By exploring its customizable features and taking advantage of the handwriting-to-text conversion, you're not just using a stylus—you're embracing a tool that adapts to your lifestyle and enhances your productivity.

Experiment with different settings, practice your gestures, and soon you'll find that the S Pen becomes an indispensable part of your daily routine. Whether you're sketching ideas, editing documents, or simply navigating your device with a flourish, the S Pen is designed to make your digital experience more natural and intuitive.

Air Actions and Shortcuts

Imagine controlling your Galaxy S25 Ultra without even touching the screen—just a few subtle gestures and taps with your S Pen, and you're navigating, capturing moments, and accessing your favorite apps in an instant.

The Magic of Air Actions

Air Actions allow you to interact with your device from a slight distance, giving you a sense of control that feels almost futuristic. Here's what makes them so remarkable:

- **Effortless Navigation:** With a simple flick or twist of the S Pen in mid-air, you can scroll through photos, switch between apps, or even control media playback. It's like having a remote control at your fingertips—no need to touch the screen.

- **Hands-Free Efficiency:** Whether you're cooking, presenting, or simply on the move, Air Actions let you operate your device without interrupting your flow. Imagine pausing your music, advancing a slideshow, or taking a snapshot during a video call—all without a single tap.

- **Seamless Integration:** The Galaxy S25 Ultra is designed to recognize a variety of gestures, meaning that whether you're swiping, tilting, or pointing, your device responds in a way that feels both natural and intuitive.

Customizing Your Air Actions

The beauty of the S Pen lies in its adaptability. You can tailor Air Actions to suit your style and daily needs:

- **Easy Setup:** Head into the S Pen settings within your device's menu. Here, you can view the available gestures and see what each one does by default. From there, it's easy to experiment and find the combination that works best for you.

- **Personal Touch:** Don't hesitate to assign specific functions to particular gestures. For example, you might configure a leftward swipe to rewind music or a quick upward flick to capture a screenshot. This personalization makes your device feel uniquely yours.

- **Sensitivity and Responsiveness:** Adjust the sensitivity of the S Pen to match your natural hand movements. A well-calibrated pen means every gesture is recognized accurately, reducing frustration and making your interactions smooth.

Unlocking the Power of Shortcuts

Beyond gestures, the S Pen's built-in button offers another layer of control. Shortcuts empower you to perform tasks quickly without ever navigating through menus:

- **Instant Actions:** With a press of the S Pen button, you can launch your camera, open your favorite note-taking app, or even trigger a specific function like "screen off memo." It's all about reducing steps and saving time.

- **Tailored to You:** Similar to Air Actions, shortcuts can be customized. Imagine setting a shortcut for checking your schedule or sending a pre-written message—all activated with a simple press. The flexibility allows you to create a workflow that matches your day-to-day activities.

- **Streamlined Workflow:** These shortcuts aren't just about speed; they're about efficiency. Whether you're in the middle of a creative session or multitasking during a hectic day, having essential actions a button press away means fewer interruptions and more focus on what matters.

Bringing It All Together: Real-World Applications

Let's put these features into context with some practical examples:

- **During a Presentation:** Use Air Actions to swipe between slides without being tethered to your device, while the S Pen's shortcut button can quickly toggle your presenter notes.

- **Photography on the Fly:** Capture the perfect shot by using a simple gesture to control the camera, or set up a shortcut for instant access to different shooting modes.

- **Everyday Convenience:** Whether you're cooking, exercising, or simply lounging, imagine using a quick S Pen gesture to adjust the volume, switch playlists, or even send a text—all while your hands remain free.

Tips and Best Practices

- **Experiment Freely:** The best way to master these features is by trying them out in different scenarios. Don't worry about making mistakes; every gesture you try is a step toward a more personalized experience.

- **Keep It Simple:** While there's a wide array of actions available, focus on the ones that genuinely enhance your routine. Start small, then expand your repertoire as you become more comfortable.

- **Stay Updated:** Samsung frequently updates its software, adding new gestures and customization options. Keeping your device updated ensures you always have the latest features and improvements at your fingertips.

Air Actions and Shortcuts redefine the way you interact with your Galaxy S25 Ultra. They turn your S Pen into a dynamic tool—one that adapts to your lifestyle, simplifies everyday tasks, and empowers you to engage with technology in a truly intuitive way. Embrace these features, experiment with different gestures and shortcuts, and soon you'll find that managing your device has never been so effortless or fun.

Take a moment to explore these capabilities, and watch as your digital world transforms into an extension of your creativity and efficiency. Happy gesturing!

CHAPTER SIX

Camera and Photography Tips

Welcome to the world of photography on your Galaxy S25 Ultra! In this chapter, we'll explore the various camera modes and settings that turn everyday moments into stunning works of art. Whether you're an amateur photographer looking to capture memories or a pro seeking to push creative boundaries, this guide will help you harness the full power of your device's camera.

Exploring Camera Modes

Your Galaxy S25 Ultra comes equipped with a rich array of camera modes, each designed to capture different scenes and lighting conditions effortlessly. Let's take a closer look:

- **Auto Mode:** For everyday shots, the Auto Mode is your reliable companion. The camera automatically adjusts settings like exposure, focus, and color balance, so you can snap beautiful photos without any fuss. It's perfect for quick captures when you don't have time to tweak the settings manually.

- **Pro Mode:** For those moments when you want complete control, Pro Mode lets you fine-tune every element—

from shutter speed and ISO to white balance and focus. This mode is ideal for creative photography and challenging lighting conditions. Experimenting here can transform a simple snapshot into a professional-quality image.

- **Night Mode:** When the sun goes down, Night Mode steps in to ensure your photos shine even in low light. By using longer exposure times and advanced noise reduction techniques, Night Mode captures vibrant details that other phones might miss. It's your go-to for cityscapes, starry skies, or any scenario where light is scarce.

- **Portrait Mode:** This mode is designed to make your subjects stand out. Using depth-of-field technology, Portrait Mode creates a beautifully blurred background, emphasizing the subject and adding a professional touch to your portraits. It's perfect for selfies, group photos, and capturing those candid moments.

- **Ultra Wide and Macro Modes:** Expand your creative possibilities with Ultra Wide for expansive landscapes or tight spaces, and Macro Mode for those up-close shots where every tiny detail matters. These specialized modes allow you to capture perspectives that are simply not possible with a standard lens.

Tweaking Camera Settings for Perfection

While the different modes offer tailored experiences, adjusting the camera settings can further elevate your photography. Here's how to get the best out of your device:

- **Resolution and Aspect Ratio:** Choose the right resolution and aspect ratio for your needs. Whether you're capturing moments for social media or preparing high-resolution prints, adjusting these settings ensures your photos look their best on any platform.

- **Focus and Exposure:** In Pro Mode, manual focus lets you zero in on exactly what matters most in your frame. Similarly, controlling the exposure helps manage light in challenging environments. Experiment with these settings to create the perfect balance of brightness and detail.

- **HDR and Filters:** High Dynamic Range (HDR) is a powerful feature for scenes with a wide range of light intensities. It combines multiple exposures to create a balanced image that captures both the bright highlights and the deep shadows. And if you want to add a creative flair, explore the built-in filters that can instantly transform the mood of your photo.

- **Timer and Burst Modes:** The timer is handy for group shots or self-portraits, giving you the chance to be part of the frame. Burst mode, on the other hand, lets you capture rapid sequences, ensuring you never miss the perfect moment, whether it's a fast-moving subject or an unpredictable action shot.

- **Stabilization:** With built-in optical and electronic stabilization, your Galaxy S25 Ultra minimizes blur even in challenging conditions. This is especially useful for video recording or when capturing photos in low light. A steady hand, combined with these features, can make a world of difference in your final image.

Bringing Your Vision to Life

The beauty of the Galaxy S25 Ultra lies not just in its advanced hardware but in its ability to empower you as a storyteller. Here are a few tips to make your photography journey even more enjoyable:

- **Practice and Experiment:** Don't be afraid to experiment with different modes and settings. Photography is all about trial and error—each adjustment is a step towards mastering your craft.

- **Learn from Each Shot:** Take a moment to review your photos and learn what worked and what didn't. Whether it's the way a particular light setting brought out the colors or how a specific focus mode made a portrait pop, every shot is an opportunity to improve.

- **Share and Connect:** Photography is also about sharing your perspective with the world. Use your Galaxy S25

Ultra to capture moments that resonate with you, and share them with friends, family, or a community of like-minded enthusiasts.

Shooting in 200MP Mode

This incredible setting transforms everyday photography into an art form by capturing breathtaking detail and clarity in every shot.

What is 200MP Mode?

The 200MP mode is a game changer for photography enthusiasts. It allows you to capture images with an astonishing level of detail—perfect for landscapes, macro shots, or any moment where you want every tiny nuance preserved. With this mode, your Galaxy S25 Ultra doesn't just take pictures; it creates digital canvases filled with rich textures and vibrant details that are ready for both creative editing and large-scale printing.

Activating 200MP Mode

Getting started with 200MP mode is simple, yet it comes with a few key considerations:

- **Access the Camera App:** Open your Galaxy S25 Ultra's camera app and switch to the high-resolution mode. You might see an icon or option labeled "200MP"—tap it to activate the mode.

- **Ensure Adequate Lighting:** Although the 200MP mode excels in detail, it works best in well-lit conditions. Natural light helps capture the true colors and finer details of your subject.

- **Storage Considerations:** Because 200MP images are large, make sure you have enough storage space available. Consider using a microSD card or cloud backup to keep your high-resolution masterpieces safe.

Best Practices for Shooting in 200MP Mode

To truly harness the power of 200MP photography, here are some tips and tricks:

- **Stability is Key:** With such high resolution, even the slightest shake can affect your image. Use a tripod or steady your hands to avoid blur, especially in low-light conditions.

- **Mind Your Composition:** The clarity offered by 200MP mode allows you to crop and edit images without losing detail. However, a well-thought-out composition from the start will save you time in post-processing and lead to more impactful images.

- **Experiment with Different Subjects:** From sweeping landscapes to intricate textures and tiny details in nature, try capturing a variety of subjects. Each scene can reveal something new when viewed through a 200MP lens.

- **Use Burst Mode for Action Shots:** When photographing moving subjects, burst mode can help you catch the perfect moment. This ensures you have multiple high-resolution images to choose from.

Advantages and Considerations

While the benefits of 200MP mode are compelling, there are a few considerations to keep in mind:

- **Unmatched Detail:** The high resolution lets you zoom in on images with minimal loss of clarity—ideal for prints and detailed edits.

- **Larger File Sizes:** Be prepared for larger image files, which might take up more storage space and require robust post-processing software.

- **Battery Usage:** Shooting in 200MP mode can be more demanding on your battery. It's a good idea to keep your device charged or carry a portable power bank during long shoots.

- **Not Always Necessary:** For everyday snaps or social media posts, a lower resolution might be more practical. Save 200MP mode for those moments when you really want to capture every detail.

Post-Processing and Sharing Your 200MP Masterpieces

After capturing your high-resolution photos, post-processing can enhance their impact even further:

- **Editing Software:** Use photo editing apps like Adobe Lightroom or Snapseed that can handle large files to adjust colors, sharpness, and contrast. These tools help you bring out the best in your images.

- **Organizing Your Photos:** Given their size, it's essential to organize your 200MP photos efficiently. Create dedicated folders or use cloud storage solutions to manage your portfolio.

- **Sharing Online:** When sharing online, consider the platform's resolution limits. You may need to resize or compress your photos slightly, but always keep a full-resolution version for printing or future editing.

Shooting in 200MP mode on your Galaxy S25 Ultra is like having a professional-grade camera in your pocket. It opens up a realm of creative possibilities, allowing you to capture life with unprecedented clarity and detail. Whether you're a seasoned photographer or just starting to explore your creative side, embrace this mode as a tool to experiment, learn, and elevate your photography to new heights.

Pro Video and Editing Tips

Let's explore how to leverage the advanced Pro Video mode to capture cinematic moments and then polish them with smart editing tips. Whether you're filming your next travel vlog, a family gathering, or a creative project, these insights will help you produce videos that look and feel professional.

Getting Started with Pro Video Mode

Your Galaxy S25 Ultra's Pro Video mode offers a suite of manual controls that let you take charge of your video settings. Here's how to make the most of it:

- **Accessing Pro Video Mode:** Open your camera app and switch to Pro Video mode. This setting unlocks a range of options like manual focus, adjustable shutter speed, ISO, and white balance. These controls empower you to tailor each shot according to the environment and your creative vision.

- **Fine-Tuning Your Settings:** Experiment with manual adjustments to find the perfect balance. For instance, lowering the shutter speed in low-light situations can create beautiful light trails, while adjusting the ISO helps maintain clarity without introducing unwanted noise. It's all about fine-tuning until your video reflects the mood and detail you want.

- **Stabilization is Key:** When shooting high-quality video, stability makes all the difference. Utilize a tripod or a gimbal to minimize shake, ensuring that your footage is smooth and professional. Your Galaxy S25 Ultra's built-in stabilization works wonders, but extra support can elevate your results even further.

- **Framing and Composition:** Use grid lines to help you maintain proper framing and balance in every shot. Whether you're capturing a wide landscape or a close-up scene, composition plays a vital role in making your video visually appealing. Don't be afraid to move around and try different angles—the more you experiment, the better your eye becomes for storytelling.

Tips for Shooting Like a Pro

Once you're comfortable with Pro Video mode, here are some practical tips to enhance your filming experience:

- **Plan Your Shots:** Think of your video as a series of scenes. Storyboard your ideas, or at least have a clear vision of the beginning, middle, and end. This planning helps you capture consistent and cohesive footage.

- **Mind the Audio:** Great video isn't just about visuals. Ensure that your audio is crisp by testing built-in mics or, if possible, using an external microphone. Clear audio can significantly elevate the overall quality of your video.

- **Lighting Matters:** Good lighting is essential for professional-looking videos. Whether you're shooting indoors or outdoors, use natural light to your advantage or supplement with portable lights. Keep an eye on shadows and highlights to avoid unwanted distractions.

- **Capture More Than You Need:** Record extra footage whenever possible. This gives you more options during editing and ensures you won't miss that perfect moment. Use burst recording or slow-motion features to add variety and drama to your scenes.

Editing Your Video for a Polished Finish

After capturing your footage, editing is where your story truly comes to life. The Galaxy S25 Ultra offers powerful editing tools, both built-in and compatible with external apps, to help you refine your work:

- **Built-In Video Editor:** Start with the native editor in your Gallery app. Trim clips, adjust the pace, and add transitions to create a smooth narrative flow. The intuitive interface makes it easy to experiment with different sequences until you find what works best.

- **Color Correction and Filters:** Fine-tune your video's mood with color correction tools. Adjust brightness, contrast, and saturation to enhance the visual appeal. Apply filters sparingly to add a unique style without overpowering the natural colors of your footage.

- **Sound Design:** Synchronize background music, adjust audio levels, or add voice-overs to complement your visuals. Good sound design not only enriches the viewing experience but also sets the tone of your video.

- **Exporting and Sharing:** Once you're satisfied with your edits, choose the appropriate resolution and format for your intended audience. Whether you're uploading to social media or archiving a masterpiece, ensure that your export settings maintain the high quality of your original footage.

- **Experiment with Third-Party Apps:** If you're looking for more advanced features, consider exploring apps like Adobe Premiere Rush or other mobile video editors. These tools offer additional effects, detailed timeline editing, and more nuanced control over your final product.

Bringing It All Together

Pro Video mode and smart editing are more than just technical features—they're the keys to unlocking your creative potential. Every setting you adjust, every shot you capture, and every edit you make is a step toward telling your story in a way that's uniquely yours. The Galaxy S25 Ultra empowers you to experiment fearlessly, turning everyday moments into cinematic memories.

Take your time, practice your techniques, and enjoy the process of learning. With each video you create, you'll not only improve your technical skills but also discover new ways to express your creativity. So, grab your Galaxy S25 Ultra, light up your scene, and let your story unfold one frame at a time.

Happy filming and editing!

CHAPTER SEVEN

Security and Privacy Features

In today's digital age, protecting your personal data is more important than ever. The Galaxy S25 Ultra is designed with a suite of advanced security features that not only guard your information but also make unlocking and organizing your device a seamless experience. In this chapter, we'll explore how Face Recognition and Fingerprint Security work together to keep your device secure, and how Secure Folder along with Knox Security offers a fortress for your sensitive data.

Face Recognition and Fingerprint Security

Imagine a security system that recognizes you instantly—no more fumbling with passwords or PINs. With the Galaxy S25 Ultra, you have two powerful biometric options at your disposal:

- **Face Recognition:** This feature uses advanced technology to analyze your facial features quickly and accurately. Simply look at your device, and it unlocks in an instant. It's designed to work in various lighting conditions, ensuring you get fast, secure access whether you're indoors or out. Plus, it adds a personal touch to your device, making it truly yours.

- **Fingerprint Security:** For those moments when you prefer a tactile method of authentication, the fingerprint sensor is there to help. Located conveniently on the screen or the back of the device (depending on your model), this sensor reads the unique patterns of your fingerprint with remarkable precision. It's fast, reliable, and incredibly easy to set up. By simply placing your finger on the sensor, you gain secure access to your phone, your apps, and even sensitive files.

Together, these biometric features ensure that only you can unlock your device, providing a strong layer of protection that's both user-friendly and highly secure.

Secure Folder and Knox Security

Beyond unlocking your device, keeping your personal files, photos, and documents secure is a top priority. That's where Secure Folder and Knox Security come in:

- **Secure Folder:** Think of the Secure Folder as your private vault within your Galaxy S25 Ultra. Here, you can store sensitive data like confidential documents, personal photos, and secure apps away from prying eyes. With its intuitive interface, you can easily move files into the Secure Folder and access them using your preferred authentication method—be it face recognition, fingerprint, or a PIN. It's a simple yet effective way to separate your private information from the rest of your device.

- **Knox Security:** Underpinning the entire security framework of your Galaxy S25 Ultra is Knox Security. This multi-layered protection system works at the hardware and software levels to detect and fend off potential threats. Knox continuously monitors your device for unusual activity and keeps your data safe with real-time protection. Whether you're shopping online, accessing sensitive emails, or just browsing, Knox is there to ensure your digital world remains secure.

By combining the ease of Secure Folder with the robust protection of Knox Security, your Galaxy S25 Ultra creates a secure environment that is tailored to your personal and professional needs.

Embracing the advanced security and privacy features of your Galaxy S25 Ultra means you can focus on what matters most—staying connected and productive—without worrying about the safety of your personal data. With Face Recognition and Fingerprint Security, you unlock your device quickly and confidently, while Secure Folder and Knox Security provide peace of mind by safeguarding your most sensitive information.

Managing App Permissions

In a world where our smartphones hold more personal information than ever before, managing app permissions is a critical step in keeping your data secure and your privacy intact. Your Galaxy S25 Ultra offers intuitive controls that let you decide what information each app can access, so you stay in charge of your digital life.

Understanding App Permissions

Every app on your phone asks for permission to access certain features or data—whether it's your location, contacts, or camera. These permissions are essential for apps to function properly, but they can also be gateways to your personal information if left unchecked.

- **What Are App Permissions?** App permissions are settings that determine what parts of your phone an app can interact with. They help maintain a balance between functionality and privacy.

- **Why They Matter:** By managing these permissions, you ensure that each app only accesses what it really needs.

This not only protects your personal data but also minimizes potential vulnerabilities.

Navigating Your Permission Settings

Your Galaxy S25 Ultra makes it simple to review and control permissions for every app. Here's how you can get started:

- **Accessing App Permissions:**

    o Open the **Settings** menu on your device.

    o Navigate to **Apps** or **Applications**.

    o Look for an option like **App Permissions** or **Permission Manager**. This section gives you an overview of all the permissions that apps have requested.

- **Reviewing Permissions by Category:** Permissions are typically grouped into categories such as Camera, Location, Microphone, Contacts, and more. This organization lets you quickly see which apps have access to sensitive data.

- **Detailed App Insights:** Tap on a specific permission category to see a list of apps that have requested that access. You can then decide if an app truly needs that permission or if it's time to revoke it.

Customizing Your Permissions

Taking control of your privacy means adjusting permissions to match your comfort level. Here are some steps to tailor your device settings:

- **Granting or Revoking Access:** For each app, you can toggle permissions on or off based on your preferences. If you notice an app with unnecessary access to your location or contacts, simply switch it off.

  - For instance, a simple game might not need to access your contacts—so why give it permission?

- **Temporary Permissions:** Some apps allow you to grant temporary access. This means they can use a feature only while the app is in use, adding an extra layer of protection.

- **Handling Updates:** When apps update, they might request new permissions. Keep an eye out for these prompts and evaluate if the new permissions make sense for the app's functionality.

Best Practices for Managing Permissions

Staying on top of your app permissions is an ongoing process. Here are a few tips to help you maintain a secure environment:

- **Regular Reviews:** Make it a habit to review your permissions periodically. A quick check can help you catch any changes or new apps that might have more access than you're comfortable with.

- **Be Skeptical of Unnecessary Requests:** If an app asks for permissions that seem irrelevant to its function—like a flashlight app requesting access to your contacts—it might be best to deny that access or consider an alternative app.

- **Educate Yourself:** Familiarize yourself with what each permission entails. Knowing the difference between "allow while using the app" versus "always allow" can help you make smarter decisions.

- **Use Secure Folder for Sensitive Apps:** For apps that handle particularly sensitive data, consider using Samsung's Secure Folder. This adds another layer of protection, keeping your important information in a separate, secure space.

The Bigger Picture: Why It All Matters

Managing app permissions is more than just a technical tweak—it's about reclaiming control over your personal data. With every permission you review and adjust, you're building a digital fortress that shields your privacy from unnecessary exposure. In today's connected world, that peace of mind is invaluable.

Your Galaxy S25 Ultra is designed with powerful tools that empower you to decide who gets access to your personal information. By actively managing app permissions, you're not just protecting your data—you're taking an important step toward a safer, more secure mobile experience.

Take a few moments to explore these settings on your device. The process is simple, and the benefits are profound. With your privacy in your hands, you can enjoy all the innovative features of your Galaxy S25 Ultra without compromise.

Stay secure, stay informed, and let your smartphone work for you—safely and smartly.

CHAPTER EIGHT

Customization and Personalization

Your Galaxy S25 Ultra isn't just a smartphone—it's an extension of your personality. With a range of customization options, you can make your device truly your own. In this chapter, we'll explore how to transform your home screen using themes, wallpapers, and widgets, creating a space that's as unique and dynamic as you are.

Themes: Express Your Style

Themes are like a wardrobe for your phone. They allow you to change the look and feel of your device with just a few taps. Here's how you can explore and personalize your Galaxy S25 Ultra with themes:

- **Transform the Overall Look:** Choose from a variety of themes that change your icons, colors, and even system fonts. Whether you prefer a sleek, minimalist design or a vibrant, eye-catching style, there's a theme that fits your personality.

- **Easy Customization:** Samsung's theme store offers both free and premium options, letting you experiment with different styles without any hassle. Simply browse

83

through the available themes, preview them on your device, and apply the one that resonates with you.

- **Seasonal and Event-Based Options:** Keep an eye out for special themes during holidays or events. These limited-edition designs can add a fun, timely twist to your phone's appearance, keeping your device feeling fresh and exciting.

Wallpapers: Set the Perfect Backdrop

Wallpapers are the canvas of your home screen, providing the perfect backdrop for your apps and widgets. Here's how to select and personalize your wallpapers:

- **Reflect Your Personality:** Choose a wallpaper that speaks to you—whether it's a breathtaking landscape, a piece of abstract art, or a personal photo that holds special memories. Your wallpaper is the first thing you see, so let it set the tone for your daily digital experience.

- **Dynamic and Live Wallpapers:** For an added touch of interactivity, try dynamic or live wallpapers. These backgrounds move subtly or change based on your device's settings, adding a layer of depth and life to your screen without overwhelming it.

- **Easy Adjustments:** The Galaxy S25 Ultra makes it simple to switch wallpapers. Dive into your settings or use the customization menu to rotate your wallpapers periodically. It's a small change that can keep your device feeling new and inspiring.

Widgets: Quick Access and Personal Touch

Widgets are your home screen's power-ups—they give you instant access to information and functionality, all at a glance. Here's how to make the most of widgets on your device:

- **Instant Information:** From weather updates and news feeds to calendar events and to-do lists, widgets bring the information you need directly to your home screen. This means you're always one glance away from what matters most, without needing to open an app.

- **Customizable Layout:** Arrange your widgets to create a layout that suits your workflow. Whether you prefer a clean, minimalist setup or a more detailed dashboard, you can resize and position widgets to craft a home screen that works best for you.

- **Mix and Match:** Experiment with different combinations of widgets. Perhaps a clock widget paired with your favorite news feed and a photo slideshow creates the perfect balance of function and personality. The flexibility is endless, allowing your home screen to evolve with your needs.

Customization and personalization aren't just about aesthetics—they're about creating an environment that feels uniquely yours. By mixing themes, wallpapers, and widgets, you can transform your Galaxy S25 Ultra into a personal digital haven that reflects your style, enhances your productivity, and keeps you inspired every time you unlock your device.

Mastering the Always-On Display

One of the standout features of the Galaxy S25 Ultra is the **Always-On Display (AOD)**—a simple yet powerful way to keep important information visible without fully waking your phone. Whether you want to check the time, see your notifications at a glance, or add a personal touch with custom graphics, the AOD gives you a world of options.

What Is the Always-On Display?

The Always-On Display is a feature that keeps certain parts of your screen active even when your phone is locked. Unlike the traditional lock screen, AOD uses minimal power to display **the time, date, battery percentage, notifications, and even custom widgets or images**. This means you don't have to tap your phone just to check the time or see if you've missed an important message.

How to Enable and Customize the Always-On Display

Samsung gives you plenty of ways to tweak the AOD to match your style. To enable and customize it:

1. **Go to Settings** → Select **Lock Screen & Always-On Display**

2. **Tap Always-On Display** to turn it on

3. Choose **when you want it to appear**:

    o **Tap to Show:** Display stays off until you tap the screen

    o **Show Always:** AOD stays on at all times (uses more battery)

    o **Show on Schedule:** Only displays at specific times of the day

    o **Show for New Notifications:** Appears only when you have new messages or alerts

Once enabled, you can start customizing the look and feel of your AOD.

Customizing the AOD Clock, Colors, and Styles

The AOD isn't just about functionality—it's also a fun way to express yourself. Samsung offers plenty of design options:

- **Clock Styles:** Choose from digital, analog, or even a playful custom design

- **Colors:** Pick a color scheme that suits your vibe

- **Widgets:** Add weather updates, calendar events, or music controls

- **GIFs and Custom Images:** Make your AOD more lively with an animated GIF or your favorite picture

To customize these:

1. **Go to Settings → Lock Screen & Always-On Display**

2. Tap **Clock Style** or **AOD Settings**

3. Browse through the available options and select what fits your preference

AOD Widgets: More Than Just a Clock

Did you know you can add widgets to your Always-On Display? These mini-utilities let you access **music controls, upcoming calendar events, and even your daily step count** without unlocking your phone.

To enable AOD widgets:

1. **Go to Settings → Lock Screen & Always-On Display**

2. Scroll down and tap **Widgets**

3. Choose which widgets you want to enable

Once activated, you can toggle through them by double-tapping the AOD screen.

Battery Impact: Does AOD Drain Your Battery?

A common concern is whether the Always-On Display affects battery life. The good news is that **Samsung has optimized AOD to use minimal power**—especially with the Galaxy S25 Ultra's **efficient AMOLED display**. Since only individual pixels light up, the power consumption is much lower than waking the entire screen.

To **minimize battery usage** while still enjoying AOD:

- Use **Tap to Show** instead of "Show Always"

- Reduce brightness or choose a **simpler clock design**

- Set a **schedule** so AOD turns off during sleep hours

The Always-On Display is more than just a passive clock—it's a feature that **saves you time, enhances convenience, and adds a personal touch to your phone**. Whether you prefer a simple digital clock, an animated GIF, or a full suite of widgets, the Galaxy S25 Ultra gives you the flexibility to make AOD work for you.

Edge Panels and Multi-Tasking

Your Galaxy S25 Ultra is designed not only to keep you connected but also to empower you to tailor your experience exactly how you like it. Two of the most exciting ways to do that are through Edge Panels and Multi-Tasking features.

Discovering Edge Panels

Edge Panels are like your personal shortcut hub, accessible with a simple swipe from the side of your screen. They're designed to give you quick access to apps, contacts, and information without having to dig through your home screen.

- **What Are Edge Panels?** Edge Panels let you display a vertical bar of widgets and shortcuts along the edge of your screen. Whether it's your favorite apps, quick contacts, or tools like the calculator and calendar, everything you need can be just a swipe away.

- **Customizing Your Edge Panels:** You have the power to decide which panels appear and in what order. Navigate to your settings, tap on **Display** or **Edge Screen**, and choose the panels that best suit your workflow. You can:

  - **Add/Remove Panels:** Pick and choose the content that matters most to you.

  - **Reorder Panels:** Arrange them so that the apps or shortcuts you use most frequently are always at your fingertips.

  - **Personalize Content:** Some panels even let you add custom shortcuts, so your favorite contacts, recent documents, or frequently used tools are instantly accessible.

- **Why They Matter:** Edge Panels help you stay organized and efficient. They cut down on time wasted searching for apps and information, and they create a more intuitive, streamlined user experience. Imagine being able to launch your music player, check your schedule, or quickly call a friend—all with one swift motion.

Mastering Multi-Tasking

Multi-tasking on the Galaxy S25 Ultra isn't just about running two apps at once—it's about creating a dynamic workspace that adapts to your needs. With the advanced multi-window features, you can boost your productivity and enjoy a more fluid user experience.

- **Multi-Window Mode:** This feature lets you run two apps side-by-side. Whether you're browsing the web while taking notes, watching a video during a video call, or keeping an eye on your calendar while replying to emails, multi-window mode ensures that you can do more at once.

    o **How to Activate:** Open the recent apps view and tap the multi-window icon on the app you want to use. Then, select another app to join it in a split-screen layout.

    o **Adjusting the Layout:** You can drag the divider to give one app more screen space. It's all about finding the right balance to suit your task.

- **Pop-Up View and Floating Windows:** For those moments when you need quick access without switching away from your current app, Pop-Up View is a game changer. This feature lets you open an app in a smaller window that hovers over your screen.

  - **Customizing Pop-Up View:** Resize or move these windows as needed so that they don't disrupt your workflow. It's perfect for checking messages, viewing directions, or even monitoring social media while you work on something else.

- **Benefits of Enhanced Multi-Tasking:** With multi-tasking, you can turn your Galaxy S25 Ultra into a portable workstation. It allows for:

  - **Efficient Workflow:** Seamlessly switch between tasks without losing context.

  - **Greater Productivity:** Manage multiple tasks at once, saving time and reducing the need to constantly toggle between apps.

  - **A Personalized Experience:** Arrange your apps and windows in a way that mirrors your work style, whether it's for productivity, entertainment, or creative projects.

Bringing It All Together

Customizing your Galaxy S25 Ultra through Edge Panels and Multi-Tasking features isn't just about having more functionality—it's about creating a digital space that feels uniquely yours. With Edge Panels, you can streamline access to the apps and information you rely on daily, and with Multi-Tasking, you can handle multiple projects at once without missing a beat.

- **Experiment and Evolve:** The beauty of these features is their flexibility. Take some time to experiment with different panel setups and multi-window arrangements. As your daily routine evolves, so too can your settings.

- **Stay Organized, Stay Efficient:** By setting up your device in a way that mirrors your personal workflow, you'll save time and reduce stress, leaving you free to focus on what matters most—whether that's work, creativity, or leisure.

- **Your Personalized Digital Hub:** Remember, your smartphone is more than just a tool—it's a reflection of you. Use Edge Panels and Multi-Tasking to make your Galaxy S25 Ultra an extension of your personality and a catalyst for your daily success.

The Galaxy S25 Ultra is built to adapt to your life, not the other way around. By harnessing the power of Edge Panels and Multi-Tasking, you're not only enhancing your device's functionality but also making it truly your own. Enjoy the process of personalization, and watch as your smartphone transforms into a personalized command center that's perfectly aligned with your lifestyle.

Happy customizing and multi-tasking!

CHAPTER NINE

Battery Management and Performance Optimization

Your Galaxy S25 Ultra is a technological marvel, but to keep it performing at its best, a little care goes a long way. This chapter is all about making smart choices to preserve your battery life, optimize your device's performance, and ensure your smartphone stays efficient through every busy day. Let's dive into some practical tips on the best charging practices, making the most of battery saver modes, and keeping your RAM and storage in check.

Best Charging Practices

A well-cared-for battery means longer-lasting performance and less hassle over time. Here are some friendly tips to help you get the most out of your Galaxy S25 Ultra's battery:

- **Stick with the Right Charger:** Always use the official Samsung charger or a high-quality USB-C charger that meets the proper specifications. This ensures that your device charges safely and efficiently.

- **Mind the Temperature:** Extreme heat or cold can harm your battery. Avoid charging your phone in direct sunlight or in freezing conditions. Keeping your device at a moderate temperature helps maintain battery health.

- **Smart Charging Habits:** Aim to keep your battery between 20% and 80% most of the time. Although it's fine to charge to 100% when needed, doing it daily can gradually wear down the battery. Samsung's "Battery Protection" setting even allows you to limit charging to around 85%, which is great for long-term health.

- **Avoid Constant Overnight Charging:** While modern smartphones have safeguards, leaving your phone plugged in all night can sometimes lead to trickle charging and extra heat. If possible, try to unplug once it's fully charged, or take advantage of features like Adaptive Battery that manage overnight charging intelligently.

Battery Saver Modes

There are times when you need every bit of power you can get—whether you're traveling, in a meeting, or simply trying to stretch your battery life through a long day. Your Galaxy S25 Ultra comes with built-in battery saver options that can make a real difference:

- **Standard Power Saving Mode:** Activate this mode to reduce background activity, dim the screen brightness, and limit performance slightly. It's perfect for those days when you know you won't be near a charger for a while.

- **Ultra Power Saving Mode:** When your battery is running critically low, this mode kicks in to keep the essentials working. It restricts your device to core functions—like calling, texting, and basic browsing—and switches your display to grayscale to minimize power consumption.

- **Adaptive Battery:** This smart feature learns your habits over time and prioritizes battery usage for the apps you use most frequently. It also limits power to apps that run in the background but aren't used often, helping you conserve energy without even thinking about it.

- **Managing Background Apps:** In the Battery and Device Care settings, you can also restrict or put unused apps to sleep. This prevents them from draining your battery when they're not actively in use, ensuring that only the apps you need are consuming power.

RAM and Storage Optimization

Just like a well-organized desk helps you work more efficiently, keeping your RAM and storage optimized makes your Galaxy S25 Ultra run faster and smoother. Here are some tips to maintain top performance:

- **RAM Plus – Boosting Your Multitasking Power:** The Galaxy S25 Ultra features a handy tool called RAM Plus, which uses part of your storage as virtual RAM. This extra memory helps keep your apps running smoothly, especially when you're juggling multiple tasks. You can adjust the allocation in your settings, tailoring it to your usage habits.

- **Clearing Cached Data:** Over time, apps accumulate temporary files that can slow down your device. Regularly clearing the cache—either manually from individual app settings or through the Device Care section—can free up memory and boost speed.

- **Storage Maintenance:** A full storage can be like a cluttered workspace. Use the Storage Analyzer in Device Care to identify large or unused files and apps. Backing up photos and videos to Samsung Cloud or OneDrive is a great way to free up space while keeping your memories safe.

- **App Sleeping and Deep Sleep Modes:** Some apps continue to run in the background even when not needed. By placing these apps into sleep mode, you can prevent them from consuming unnecessary RAM and battery life. This is particularly useful for apps you rarely use but don't want to uninstall.

Managing your battery and optimizing performance on your Galaxy S25 Ultra isn't just about tweaking settings—it's about creating a balanced routine that keeps your device running like new. By practicing smart charging, utilizing battery saver modes when needed, and keeping your RAM and storage organized, you'll enjoy a smoother, more reliable smartphone experience every day.

Remember, a little care goes a long way. With these tips in hand, you're well on your way to maximizing the performance and longevity of your Galaxy S25 Ultra—so you can focus on what truly matters, without worrying about your device slowing you down.

Happy optimizing!

CHAPTER TEN

Common Problems and Solutions

No matter how advanced a smartphone is, occasional hiccups are inevitable. Fortunately, your Galaxy S25 Ultra comes with built-in tools and solutions to handle most issues quickly. This chapter will guide you through troubleshooting some of the most common problems, including Wi-Fi and Bluetooth connectivity issues, app crashes, and when to use factory reset or recovery mode.

Wi-Fi and Bluetooth Connectivity Issues

Problem: Your Wi-Fi won't connect, keeps dropping, or is painfully slow. Or perhaps Bluetooth won't pair with a device, disconnects unexpectedly, or doesn't work as expected.

Quick Fixes for Wi-Fi Issues

- **Toggle Wi-Fi Off and On:** The simplest fix is often the most effective. Swipe down from the top of your screen, turn off Wi-Fi, wait a few seconds, and turn it back on.

- **Restart Your Router and Phone:** If your Wi-Fi connection remains unstable, restart your router and modem. After that, restart your Galaxy S25 Ultra and try connecting again.

- **Forget and Reconnect to Wi-Fi:** If a specific network won't connect, go to *Settings > Connections > Wi-Fi*, tap the network, select *Forget*, and reconnect by entering the password.

- **Switch Between 2.4GHz and 5GHz Bands:** Some routers offer both frequency bands. If you're experiencing connectivity problems, switching to a different band might help.

- **Check for Software Updates:** Samsung regularly releases updates that improve Wi-Fi performance. Check for updates by going to *Settings > Software Update > Download and Install*.

Quick Fixes for Bluetooth Issues

- **Toggle Bluetooth Off and On:** Just like with Wi-Fi, sometimes simply turning Bluetooth off and on (*Settings > Connections > Bluetooth*) can solve the issue.

- **Forget the Device and Re-Pair:** If a Bluetooth device isn't connecting, go to *Settings > Bluetooth*, find the device, tap the settings icon, select *Forget*, then pair it again.

- **Check Device Compatibility:** Not all Bluetooth devices work with every phone. Ensure your accessory is compatible with the Galaxy S25 Ultra.

- **Reset Network Settings:** If all else fails, resetting your network settings (*Settings* > *General Management* > *Reset* > *Reset Network Settings*) can resolve persistent issues.

App Crashes and Freezing Fixes

Problem: An app keeps freezing, crashing, or lagging, making it frustrating to use.

Quick Fixes for App Issues

- **Force Stop the App:** If an app becomes unresponsive, go to *Settings* > *Apps*, find the app, and tap *Force Stop*. Then, reopen it and see if the issue persists.

- **Clear App Cache and Data:**

  o Go to *Settings* > *Apps* > *[App Name]*.

  o Tap *Storage*.

o   Select *Clear Cache* (this removes temporary files).

o   If the problem continues, tap *Clear Data* (this resets the app but may delete stored preferences or login info).

- **Check for App Updates:** Developers frequently release updates to fix bugs. Open the Google Play Store, search for the app, and update it if available.

- **Restart Your Phone:** A simple restart can clear minor software glitches. Hold the power button, then tap *Restart*.

- **Uninstall and Reinstall the App:** If the problem persists, uninstall the app and reinstall it from the Google Play Store.

Factory Reset and Recovery Mode

If your Galaxy S25 Ultra experiences persistent issues that other troubleshooting steps haven't resolved, a **factory reset** or **recovery mode** can be your last resort.

Factory Reset (When to Use It & How to Do It)

A factory reset erases all data on your device and restores it to its original state. This is useful if:

- Your phone is running extremely slow or buggy despite multiple fixes.

- You're experiencing unfixable software errors.

- You plan to sell or give away your device and want to remove all personal data.

How to Factory Reset:

1. Go to *Settings > General Management > Reset > Factory Data Reset.*

2. Review the information and tap *Reset.*

3. Enter your PIN or password if prompted.

4. Confirm by selecting *Delete All.*

Tip: Always back up your data before performing a factory reset! You can use Samsung Cloud or Google Drive to save your contacts, photos, and apps.

Recovery Mode (For Advanced Troubleshooting)

If your Galaxy S25 Ultra won't turn on or gets stuck on the Samsung logo, **Recovery Mode** can help fix it.

How to Enter Recovery Mode:

1. Turn off your device completely.

2. Press and hold the **Volume Up** and **Power** buttons simultaneously until the Samsung logo appears.

3. Use the **volume buttons** to navigate and the **power button** to select an option.

4. Choose **Wipe Cache Partition** (this removes temporary files without deleting personal data).

5. If problems persist, you may need to select **Factory Reset/Wipe Data** as a last resort.

Troubleshooting doesn't have to be stressful. By following these simple fixes, you can resolve most common problems quickly and get back to enjoying your Galaxy S25 Ultra. Whether it's a stubborn Wi-Fi connection, an unresponsive app, or a deep software issue requiring a reset, now you have the tools to keep your device running smoothly.

Remember: technology should work for you, not against you!

CONCLUSION

As we wrap up this guide, it's time to reflect on the journey you've taken with your Galaxy S25 Ultra. From setting up your device to exploring its advanced features, troubleshooting common issues, and personalizing every aspect, you're now well-equipped to navigate your smartphone like a pro. Here are some final tips and thoughts to keep you moving forward.

Final Tips and Tricks

- **Experiment Fearlessly:** Don't be afraid to try out new features and settings. The Galaxy S25 Ultra is built to adapt to your unique style—whether it's customizing your home screen, exploring pro video mode, or mastering the S Pen. Every tweak is a step toward a more personalized and efficient experience.

- **Keep It Simple:** Sometimes, the simplest solutions work best. A quick restart, a cache clear, or toggling a setting can solve many common issues. Trust in these basic troubleshooting steps—they're your first line of defense against technical hiccups.

- **Document Your Favorites:** Create a quick reference guide for the settings and tricks you find most useful.

Over time, you'll build a personal "cheat sheet" that makes your daily use even smoother.

Samsung Support and Resources

Remember, you're not alone in your tech journey. Samsung offers a wealth of resources to help you along the way:

- **Official Samsung Support:** Visit the Samsung Support website for FAQs, troubleshooting guides, and step-by-step tutorials. Whether you're facing a minor glitch or need detailed assistance, expert help is just a click away.
- **User Communities:** Engage with fellow Galaxy users through online forums, social media groups, and local tech meetups. Sharing your experiences and learning from others can provide new insights and innovative ways to use your device.
- **Retail and Service Centers:** If you ever encounter an issue that you can't resolve on your own, Samsung's authorized service centers and retail locations are available for in-person support. Don't hesitate to reach out when you need a little extra help.

Staying Updated with Software Updates

Software updates are more than just routine maintenance—they're opportunities to enhance your device's performance and security:

- **Regular Checks:** Make it a habit to check for updates in *Settings > Software Update*. Updates often bring new features, improved performance, and crucial security patches that keep your device running smoothly.
- **Automatic Updates:** Consider enabling automatic updates to ensure you never miss out on the latest enhancements. This way, your Galaxy S25 Ultra stays current with the latest innovations from Samsung.
- **Read the Release Notes:** When an update arrives, take a moment to review the release notes. Understanding what changes have been made can help you better appreciate the improvements and adapt your usage accordingly.

Your Galaxy S25 Ultra is more than just a device—it's a powerful tool that adapts to your lifestyle, fuels your creativity, and keeps you connected with the world. As you continue to explore its features and fine-tune your settings, remember that the journey of mastering technology is ongoing. Every update, every new tip, and every shared experience helps you get more out of your smartphone.

Thank you for taking the time to dive into this guide. I hope it has empowered you to use your Galaxy S25 Ultra with confidence and ease. Embrace the possibilities, keep learning, and enjoy every moment with your truly personalized digital companion.

Happy exploring!

www.ingramcontent.com/pod-product-compliance
Lightning Source LLC
LaVergne TN
LVHW052056060326
832903LV00061B/984